NATIO
GEOGR
K

PUZZLE
BOOK
TRAVEL

Published by Collins
An imprint of HarperCollins Publishers
Westerhill Road
Bishopbriggs
Glasgow G64 2QT
www.harpercollins.co.uk

HarperCollins Publishers
1st Floor, Watermarque Building, Ringsend Road, Dublin 4, Ireland

In association with National Geographic Partners, LLC

NATIONAL GEOGRAPHIC and the Yellow Border Design are trademarks of the
National Geographic Society, used under license.

First published 2018

ISBN 978-0-00-826772-8

10 9 8 7 6 5 4 3 2 1

Acknowledgements

Cover images
Hot air balloon – topseller/Shutterstock.com; Car –
Kevin Hellon/Shutterstock.com; Moped – Warut Prathaksithorn/
Shutterstock.com; Fishing boat – Thalang Itsaranggura/
Shutterstock.com; Aeroplane – ifong/Shutterstock.com; Taxi –
stocksolutions/Shutterstock.com; Rollerblades – Darrin Henry/
Shutterstock.com; Helicopter – Photos SS/Shutterstock.com;
Elephant – Talvi/Shutterstock.com

Images in order of appearance
Hot air balloon – topseller/Shutterstock.com; Aeroplane – ifong/
Shutterstock.com; Hot air balloon – topseller/Shutterstock.com;
Yacht – Vereshchagin Dmitry/Shutterstock.com; Steam train – Lipskiy
/Shutterstock.com; Taxi – Oliver Hoffmann/Shutterstock.com;
Scooter – ff olas/Shutterstock.com; Horse – Melory/Shutterstock.
com; Police Bike – kenny1/Shutterstock.com; Hot air balloon –
topseller/Shutterstock.com; Cable car – Denis Limine/Shutterstock.
com; Aeroplane – Lars Christensen/Shutterstock.com; Red Arrows –
David Fowler/Shutterstock.com; Helicopter – Photos SS/
Shutterstock.com; Glider – Aerovista Luchtfotografie/Shutterstock.
com; Sea plane – Ilia Baksheev/Shutterstock.com; Stunt planes –
Terrance Emerson/Shutterstock.com; Hot air balloon – Patrick Foto
/Shutterstock.com; Hovercraft – Coprid/Shutterstock.com; Ferry –
Netfalls Remy Musser/Shutterstock.com; Yacht – Vereshchagin
Dmitry/Shutterstock.com; Cruise ship – Roger Clark ARPS/
Shutterstock.com; Amphibious vehicle – cybercrisi/Shutterstock.
com; Submarine – xavier gallego morell/Shutterstock.com; Jet ski
– Eddie Phantana/Shutterstock.com; Junk ship – Baiterek Media/
Shutterstock.com; Hovercraft – brillenstimmer/Shutterstock.com;
Yacht – freevideophotoagency/Shutterstock.com; Junk ship – Ella
Hanochi/Shutterstock.com; Jet ski – Iamkao099/Shutterstock.com;
Cruise ship – Chris Jenner/Shutterstock.com; Fishing boat –
khlongwangchao/Shutterstock.com; Speed boat – Sergiy1975/
Shutterstock.com; Fishing boat – Thalang Itsaranggura/
Shutterstock.com; Monorail – Amirul Syaidi/Shutterstock.com;
Steam train – Lipskiy/Shutterstock.com; Shovel – schab/
Shutterstock.com; Tram – Makc/Shutterstock.com; Ticket –
daseaford/Shutterstock.com; Train – Tommy Alven/Shutterstock.
com; Underground – Dean Conway/Shutterstock.com; Monorail –
Tatiana Makotra/Shutterstock.com; Steam train – Vladimir Arndt/
Shutterstock.com; Tram – Martin Lehmann/Shutterstock.com; Lorry
– Rob Wilson/Shutterstock.com; 4x4 – Maksim Toome/Shutterstock.
com; Car – Rawpixel.com/Shutterstock.com; Tuk-tuk – Noppasin/
Shutterstock.com; Double decker bus – Joe Ravi/Shutterstock.com;
Eco-friendly bus – Martin Hoscik/Shutterstock.com; Motorbike –
MiloVad/Shutterstock.com; Moped – Supertrooper/Shutterstock.
com; Bus – Chris Jenner/Shutterstock.com; Taxi – stocksolutions/
Shutterstock.com; Car – Kevin Hellon/Shutterstock.com; Van –
XPhantom/Shutterstock.com; Motorbike – Mkbiz/Shutterstock.
com; Lorry – Nikolai Tsvetkov/Shutterstock.com; Lorry – Rob
Wilson/Shutterstock.com; Van – Vereshchagin Dmitry/Shutterstock.
com; Bike – Iboo07/Shutterstock.com; Running – Ariwasabi/
Shutterstock.com; Scooter – Ljupco Smokovski/Shutterstock.com;
Kayak – andrea crisante/Shutterstock.com; Canoe – marekuliasz/
Shutterstock.com; Walking – Rawpixel.com/Shutterstock.com;
Rollerblades – Darrin Henry/Shutterstock.com; Bike – Andrey_Popov
/Shutterstock.com; Running – Samuel Borges Photography/
Shutterstock.com; Scooter – Decha Laoharuengrongkun/
Shutterstock.com; Roller Skates – igorstevanovic/Shutterstock.com;
Kayak – marekuliasz/Shutterstock.com; Canoe – marekuliasz/
Shutterstock.com; Roller Blades – Mindscape studio/Shutterstock.
com; BMX Bike – s-ts/Shutterstock.com; Elephant – Talvi/
Shutterstock.com; Horse – Melory/Shutterstock.com; Pony – Eric
Isselee/Shutterstock.com; Camel – photomaster/Shutterstock.com;
Donkey – Eric Isselee/Shutterstock.com; Yak – Daniel Prudek/
Shutterstock.com; Mule – Jopics/Shutterstock.com; Elephant Riding
Scene – Sakdinon Kadchiangsaen/Shutterstock.com; Yak – matias
planas/Shutterstock.com; Horse – bagicat/Shutterstock.com; Fire
Engine – Tim Large/Shutterstock.com; Police Car – Luca Lorenzelli/
Shutterstock.com; Police Bike – kenny1/Shutterstock.com;
Ambulance – VanderWolf Images/Shutterstock.com; Firefighter –
ivan_kislitsin/Shutterstock.com; Fire Engine – kay
roxby/Shutterstock.com; Air Rescue – Andy Lidstone/Shutterstock.
com; Lifeboat – JASPERIMAGE/Shutterstock.com; Emergency Vehicle
Scene – bh-2/Shutterstock.com; Police officer – Drop of Light/
Shutterstock.com; Police Car – Paul Wishart/Shutterstock.com;
Ambulance – 1000 Words/Shutterstock.com; Helicopter –
LandFox/Shutterstock.com

NATIONAL GEOGRAPHIC KiDS

PUZZLE BOOK

TRAVEL

FACT-PACKED FUN

CONTENTS

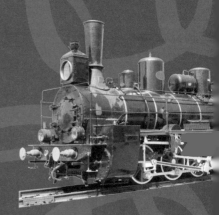

Up, up and away

Ready for take-off! Strap yourself in for fun facts and puzzles on sky-high travel over the next few pages.

The **ONLY** passengers aboard the first ever **HOT AIR BALLOON** flight were **A SHEEP, A CHICKEN,** and **A DUCK.**

CROSSWORDS

Crack the crosswords to launch the aircraft by solving the cryptic clues below. Answers have the same amount of letters as the number in brackets. Can you work out the air transport keyword using the letters in the shaded squares? See if you are right by flicking to page 90.

NASA once used two special **BOEING 747 JUMBO JETS** to carry home their **SPACE SHUTTLES** once they had returned to **EARTH.**

Across

1. Occasionally or once in a while (9)
5. Where you put rubbish (3)
7. A building in which plays are performed (7)
8. Where you go to get on an aeroplane (7)
11. Put into service (3)
12. To host guests (9)

Down

1. Material (9)
2. Flavour of most toothpastes (4)
3. Thin fog (4)
4. Nine plus eight (9)
6. Opposite of above (5)
9. Underground plant part (4)
10. Popular edible fish (4)

IN SWITZERLAND you can ride on a **DOUBLE-DECKER CABLE CAR** with an **OPEN-TOP ROOF!**

Across

1 The way a person speaks that shows where they are from (6)
5 Adult male (3)
7 Possess (3)
8 Large reptile (9)
9 Consume food (3)
10 Chemical element (3)
11 Gentle wind (6)

Down

1 The letters we use when writing (8)
2 Whole; finished (8)
3 Carry on doing something (8)
4 Get bigger in size (8)
6 Opposite of day (5)

SUDOKUS

Solve the sudokus to access the helipad. Fill in the blank squares so that numbers 1 to 6 appear once in each row, column and 3x2 box. See if you are right by flicking to page 90.

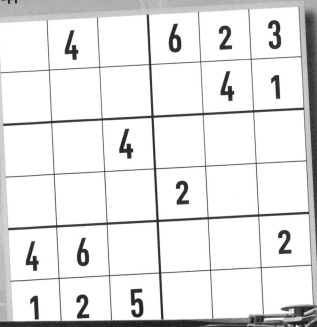

	4		6	2	3
				4	1
		4			
			2		
4	6				2
1	2	5			

HELICOPTERS get their name from the Greek word **'HELIX'**, meaning **'SPIRAL'**, because their blades go round in a **CIRCULAR MOTION.**

Wordsearches

Search the skies left to right, up and down to find the words listed in the boxes below and complete the wordsearches. See if you are right by flicking to page 90.

aeroplane
airbus
butterfly
drone

glider
jumbo jet
kite
seaplane

ZC

PH-867

s	s	o	g	c	l	t	d	s	o
a	e	g	l	i	d	e	r	b	u
e	a	b	l	l	a	l	o	u	s
r	p	p	x	d	i	r	n	t	k
o	l	q	p	i	r	a	e	t	i
p	a	j	u	m	b	o	j	e	t
l	n	o	a	o	u	w	p	r	e
a	e	m	g	t	s	l	r	f	j
n	e	b	u	h	r	r	q	l	e
e	s	s	a	a	l	e	t	y	j

GLIDERS don't have **ENGINES**, instead they use their **UNIQUE SHAPE** to help them glide through **THE SKY.**

r	b	a	l	l	o	o	n	f	e
r	s	p	a	c	e	s	h	i	p
y	o	r	s	r	t	v	d	g	b
e	p	b	l	i	m	p	a	h	j
y	p	a	r	a	c	h	u	t	e
h	e	l	i	c	o	p	t	e	r
e	a	g	l	e	g	t	r	r	d
g	b	h	t	i	w	t	c	j	c
h	a	n	g	g	l	i	d	e	r
i	t	x	r	o	c	k	e	t	d

balloon
blimp
fighter jet
hang glider
helicopter
parachute
rocket
spaceship

SEA PLANES are useful for travelling to **SMALL ISLANDS** that don't have **AIRPORTS**, because they can **LAND ON WATER!**

SPOT THE DIFFERENCE

Compare the two images of the stunt planes. Can you spot the five differences between the images? See if you are right by flicking to page 91.

See if you are right by flicking to page 91.

Before **STUNT PLANE PILOTS** can perform **IMPRESSIVE TRICKS**, they usually need over **1,000 HOURS** of flying experience.

GUESS WHAT?

Can you guess the answers to the air transport questions below?
Check your guesses by flicking to page 91.

1. What does a helicopter usually take off from and land on?
   a) Helipad
   b) Lily pad
   c) Notepad

2. What mode of transport is an airbus?
   a) Bus
   b) Aeroplane
   c) Bicycle

3. What do astronauts travel to space in?
   a) Spaceship
   b) Car
   c) Coach

4. In which area of an aeroplane would you typically find the pilot?
   a) Cockpit
   b) Cabin
   c) Galley

5. What name is given to an aircraft with no passengers that is controlled from the ground?
   a) Moan
   b) Drone
   c) Clone

6. What is a helicopter sometimes called?
   a) Cutter
   b) Slicer
   c) Chopper

7. What colours of smoke do the Red Arrows display team use?
   a) Red, green and purple
   b) Red, white and blue
   c) Black, white and red

8. Gliders are aircraft that typically do not have:
   a) Wings
   b) Pilots
   c) Engines

9. What are helicopters very good at doing that jumbo jets can't?
   a) Hovering
   b) Taking off
   c) Landing

10. Which of these brothers are famously associated with the history of flight?
    a) Wrong brothers
    b) Wright brothers
    c) White brothers

Work your way around the maze until you reach the exit.
See if you are right by flicking to page 91.

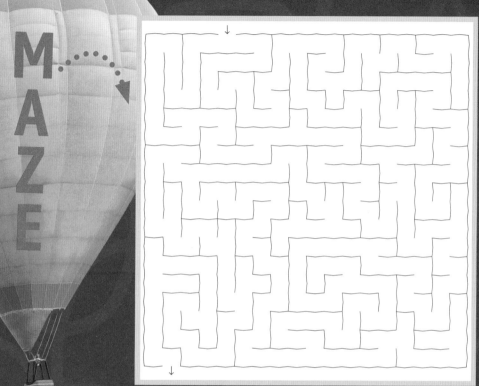

Word wheels

Can you work out the aircraft
in the two word wheels?
See if you are right by flicking to page 91.

Anchors away

Prepare to set sail for fun facts and puzzles on sea travel in this chapter.

HOVERCRAFT use **BLOWERS** to hover slightly above the **GROUND** so they can cross many **TYPES OF SURFACES.**

CROSSWORDS

Crack the crosswords by solving the cryptic clues below to release the anchors.
Answers have the same amount of letters as the number in brackets.
Can you work out the water transport keyword using the letters in the
shaded squares? See if you are right by flicking to page 92.

Most **FERRIES** carry **PEOPLE** and **CARS**, but some **SPECIAL FERRIES** even have **RAIL TRACKS** to carry **TRAINS** too.

Across

1 Country whose capital is Paris (6)
6 Stop the progress of an activity (9)
7 The end of an arm (4)
8 A desire or impulse (4)
9 Large animals with trunks (9)
11 Remained (6)

Down

1 Scare (8)
2 Was present at (8)
3 Road vehicle (3)
4 E.g. dollar or pound (8)
5 Tense or anxious (8)
10 Something worn on the head (3)

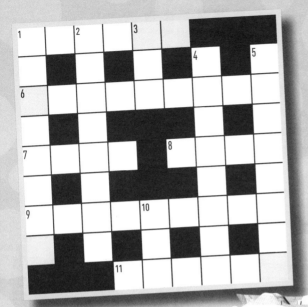

Across

1 Egypt's continent (6)
6 Not permanent (9)
7 What you are called (4)
8 Finish (4)
9 Quickest (9)
11 One of the Channel Islands (6)

Down

1 Amaze (8)
2 Recall (8)
3 Sound a dove makes (3)
4 Soft part of a bed (8)
5 Feeling of sorrow for another (8)
10 Pigment that changes the colour of something (3)

SUDOKUS

Solve the sudokus to board the ship. Fill in the blank squares so that numbers 1 to 6 appear once in each row, column and 3x2 box. See if you are right by flicking to page 92.

1	5	3	6		
		4		1	
	4	1			
			1	2	
	3		2		
		2	4	6	

The **LARGEST CRUISE SHIP** in the world weighs over **200,000 TONNES,** and can hold nearly **7,000 PASSENGERS.**

5	2		3	4	1
1					
					6
6					
				5	4
	4	5		6	3

4	5			2	1
1	6		5		
				5	
5	4				
		5		3	
2	3				5

AMPHIBIOUS VEHICLES can travel **ON LAND,** and on **(OR UNDER!) WATER** – just like **FROGS, NEWTS** and **OTHER AMPHIBIANS.**

Wordsearches

Search the seabed left to right, up and down to find the words
listed in the boxes below and complete the wordsearches.
See if you are right by flicking to page 92.

anchor

jet ski

launch

speedboat

steamship

submarine

surfboard

tugboat

vessel

yacht

SCIENTISTS can use **ROBOTIC RESEARCH SUBMARINES** to take pictures in **OCEANS** that are too deep for humans **TO EXPLORE.**

y	s	p	e	e	d	b	o	a	t
a	o	i	s	a	n	c	h	o	r
p	o	t	u	g	b	o	a	t	i
l	t	i	r	l	a	u	n	c	h
v	x	f	f	c	o	z	e	q	j
e	s	u	b	m	a	r	i	n	e
s	r	e	o	s	y	a	c	h	t
s	t	e	a	m	s	h	i	p	s
e	l	u	r	o	q	v	a	y	k
l	o	l	d	e	m	e	n	x	i

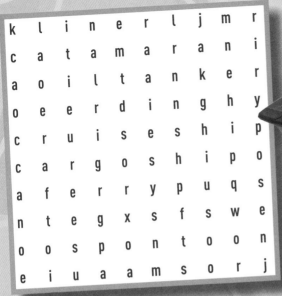

k	l	i	n	e	r	l	j	m	r
c	a	t	a	m	a	r	a	n	i
a	o	i	l	t	a	n	k	e	r
o	e	e	r	d	i	n	g	h	y
c	r	u	i	s	e	s	h	i	p
c	a	r	g	o	s	h	i	p	o
a	f	e	r	r	y	p	u	q	s
n	t	e	g	x	s	f	s	w	e
o	o	s	p	o	n	t	o	o	n
e	i	u	a	a	m	s	o	r	j

ANCIENT CHINESE JUNK SHIPS were used to explore the world in the **2ND CENTURY**, and are still used **TODAY.**

canoe
cargo ship
catamaran
cruise ship
dinghy

ferry
liner
oil tanker
pontoon
raft

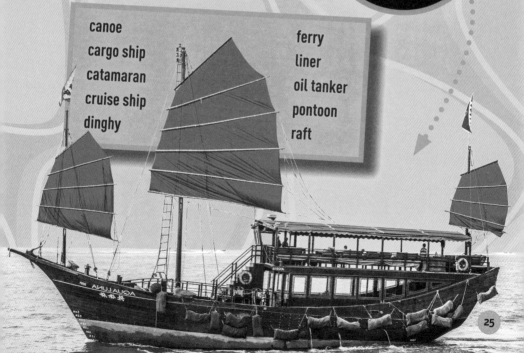

CLOSE UP

Match the mind-boggling magnifications to the named pictures opposite. See if you are right by flicking to page 93.

1

2

3

4

5

6

Hovercraft

1

Yacht

2

Junk ship

3

Jet ski

4

Cruise ship

5

6 **Fishing boat**

GUESS WHAT?

Can you guess the answers to the sea transport questions below?
Check your guesses by flicking to page 93.

1. When a submarine needs to see above water, what does it use?
   a) Periscope
   b) Telescope
   c) Goggles

2. What is the main body of a boat called?
   a) Pull
   b) Dull
   c) Hull

3. Where would you usually moor and leave a boat?
   a) Car park
   b) Garage
   c) Dock

4. Which of these does not have an engine?
   a) Kayak
   b) Motorboat
   c) Speedboat

5. What is the tall upright post on a sailing boat called?
   a) Mass
   b) Mask
   c) Mast

6. What is the back part of a boat called?
   a) Severe
   b) Stern
   c) Cross

7. Which of these vehicles is designed to transport goods from one place to another?
   a) Dinghy
   b) Raft
   c) Cargo ship

8. What is the name of a famous ship that sank in 1912?
   a) RMS Queen Mary
   b) RMS Titanic
   c) HMS Colossus

9. Which of these is able to submerge and operate underwater?
   a) Ferry
   b) Yacht
   c) Submarine

10. Which of these is a small, inflatable rubber boat?
   a) Dinghy
   b) Wherry
   c) Ferry

MAZE

Work your way around the maze until you reach the exit. See if you are right by flicking to page 93.

Word wheels

Can you work out the watercraft in the two word wheels? See if you are right by flicking to page 93.

On the tracks

Fancy a trip for fun facts and puzzles from the tracks? Get your ticket ready and set off over the next few pages for more.

Most **MONORAILS** are **ELECTRIC,** but some are powered by **MAGNETIC LEVITATION –** the **TRAINS HOVER** above the **TRACK!**

CROSSWORDS

Crack the crosswords to climb on board by solving the cryptic clues below. Answers have the same amount of letters as the number in brackets. Can you work out the track transport keyword using the letters in the shaded squares? See if you are right by flicking to page 94.

The world's **FASTEST STEAM TRAIN,** magnificent Mallard, set a **WORLD RECORD** by travelling at **126 MILES PER HOUR.**

Across
1 Reptile with sharp teeth (9)
5 Liquid often used as a fuel (3)
7 Odd (7)
8 Greet (7)
11 Tell an untruth (3)
12 Not the same (9)

Down
1 This type of puzzle (9)
2 Birds of prey that hoot (4)
3 Metallic element (4)
4 Very good (9)
6 Mistake (5)
9 Large piece of bread (4)
10 Eels (anagram) (4)

On early **STEAM TRAINS**, the **'FIREMAN'** had the job of **SHOVELLING COAL** into a firebox to power the **ENGINE**.

Across

4 Type of trousers worn in warm weather (6)
6 Narrate a story (4)
7 Clue or tip (4)
8 Female relative (4)
9 Bright object in the sky (4)
10 Number in a football team (6)

Down

1 A science (9)
2 Any animal (8)
3 Offer to do something (9)
5 Someone you do not know (8)

SUDOKUS

Solve the sudokus to get your tram ticket. Fill in the blank squares so that numbers 1 to 6 appear once in each row, column and 3x2 box. See if you are right by flicking to page 94.

6	4				
1		3			4
5			2		
		6			1
3			5		6
4				3	2

Because **TRAMS** can carry more people at once than **CARS OR BUSES**, using them causes **LESS POLLUTION.**

An **AUSTRALIAN TRAM TICKET** found in the **COAT POCKET** of a man in **LONDON** once helped **POLICE** to solve a puzzling **MURDER MYSTERY**.

Wordsearches

Complete the wordsearches so the train can disembark.
Search left to right, up and down to find the words listed in the boxes below.
See if you are right by flicking to page 94.

s	t	p	r	e	p	b	b	p	d
s	r	c	a	b	l	e	c	a	r
t	a	a	i	m	a	i	u	s	i
a	m	r	l	o	t	s	s	s	v
t	l	r	w	n	f	u	u	e	e
i	e	i	a	o	o	w	b	n	r
o	t	a	y	r	r	o	w	g	r
n	l	g	a	a	m	k	a	e	i
t	b	e	a	i	b	r	y	r	a
y	e	s	s	l	e	y	t	s	a

SHINKANSEN, also called **'BULLET TRAINS',** are high-speed **JAPANESE TRAINS** that can travel at up to **200 MILES PER HOUR!**

cable car
carriages
driver
monorail
passengers

platform
railway
station
subway
tram

r	k	t	p	u	r	u	r	s	a	s
a	s	z	s	r	l	c	t	s	o	
q	c	w	e	c	v	o	e	p	y	
i	w	q	s	i	g	n	a	l	f	
t	u	n	n	e	l	d	m	t	q	
r	j	d	w	n	g	u	a	r	d	
a	b	s	q	g	d	c	o	a	l	
c	m	r	n	i	i	t	y	v	t	
k	p	a	t	n	m	o	t	o	r	
s	m	o	k	e	p	r	h	o	n	

In **MOSCOW**, some **STRAY DOGS** have learnt how to use **TRAINS** to **TRAVEL** into the city to **FIND FOOD.**

coal

conductor

engine

guard

motor

signal

smoke

steam

tracks

tunnel

37

SPOT THE DIFFERENCE

Compare the two images of the London underground trains.
Can you spot the five differences between the images?
See if you are right by flicking to page 95.

The **LONDON UNDERGROUND** is over **150 YEARS OLD.**

GUESS WHAT?

Can you guess the answers to the track transport questions below?
Check your guesses by flicking to page 95.

1. What does a train conductor do?
   a) Take payment, check tickets and help passengers
   b) Conduct the music on board
   c) Run the coffee shop

2. What are the sections of a train usually called?
   a) Boxes
   b) Carts
   c) Carriages

3. What do overhead lines transmit to vehicles on rails?
   a) Petrol
   b) Water
   c) Electricity

4. Which of these words is an anagram of a type of passenger vehicle that runs on rails?
   a) Mart
   b) Market
   c) Shop

5. Which of these might you hear as you get on a train?
   a) 'Taxi!'
   b) 'All aboard!'
   c) 'Bingo!'

6. What underground passage might a train pass through?
   a) Burrow
   b) Flute
   c) Tunnel

7. What do trains travel on?
   a) Tracks
   b) Roads
   c) Paths

8. Where do you wait for a train?
   a) Station
   b) Bus shelter
   c) Car park

9. Which of these lets the train driver know it is safe to depart from a station?
   a) Speakers
   b) Vibrations
   c) Signals

10. Which of these was a famous early steam locomotive?
    a) Stephenson's Rocket
    b) Stephenson's Space Shuttle
    c) Stephenson's Apollo

MAZE

Work your way around the maze
until you reach the exit.
See if you are right by flicking to page 95.

Word wheels

Can you work out the railway words
in the two word wheels?
See if you are right by flicking to page 95.

Word wheel 1: R O N A M I O L

Word wheel 2: T R A N I N

Hitting the road

Buckle up and prepare for fun facts and puzzles on tarmac travel over the next few pages.

PIGS that **ESCAPED** from an **ANIMAL-TRANSPORT LORRY** in JAPAN once caused **FIVE-HOUR TRAFFIC JAMS** by TROTTING across the **ROAD.**

CROSSWORDS

Crack the crosswords to start the ignition by solving the cryptic clues below.
Answers have the same amount of letters as the number in brackets.
Can you work out the road transport keyword using the letters in the
shaded squares? See if you are right by flicking to page 96.

Because **4X4 CARS** have **FOUR ENGINE-POWERED** wheels instead of two, they can drive **OFF ROAD** or even across **SNOW.**

Across

1. Draws on (anagram) (7)
6. Chaos (5)
7. Book that lists synonyms for words (9)
8. Parts of a house (5)
9. Day off school (7)

Down

1. Tips over (9)
2. Practice session (9)
3. Many (7)
4. Obligatory or required (9)
5. Winnie-___-___ : A.A. Milne character (3, 4)

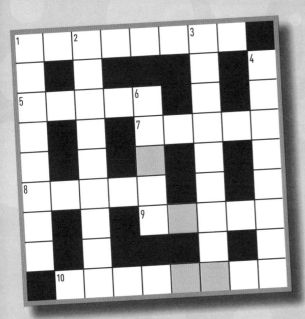

In **THAILAND, TAXIS** are called **TUK-TUKS**, and are sometimes **PEDAL-POWERED.**

Across

1 Alphabetical list of words relating to a certain subject (8)
5 Requires (5)
7 Building where people live (5)
8 On a regular basis (5)
9 Extremely precise (5)
10 A mammal with a long snout and sticky tongue (8)

Down

1 Kind and giving (8)
2 A surgical procedure (9)
3 Unwilling to do something (9)
4 Animal that hunts others (8)
6 Give out a bright light (5)

SUDOKUS

Solve the sudokus to board the double-decker. Fill in the blank squares so that numbers 1 to 6 appear once in each row, column and 3x2 box. See if you are right by flicking to page 96.

2	1	5		6	4
		4	1		
6					
					3
		1	2		6
	2		4		

BRIGHT RED, DOUBLE-DECKER BUSES are iconic in **LONDON,** and often used by **TOURISTS** to explore **THE CITY.**

4	5			6	
2					3
		4	6		5
1		5	4		
6					4
5	4				

New,
ECO-FRIENDLY ELECTRIC BUSES now have **FREE WI-FI** in some cities to **TEMPT TRAVELLERS** to use them instead of **CARS.**

			3		4
	3				2
2	4				
				4	6
1		4		6	3
6		3			1

Wordsearches

Complete the wordsearches to start your engine.
Search left to right, up and down to find the words listed in the boxes below.
See if you are right by flicking to page 96.

bus
coach
crossing
cycle lane
speed limit
taxi
toll
traffic
truck
van

a	a	t	c	i	c	o	a	c	h
t	i	s	y	a	r	i	b	r	u
n	o	p	c	e	o	a	x	m	e
p	t	o	l	l	s	r	s	t	b
e	i	i	e	m	s	a	k	r	j
r	y	e	l	o	i	t	t	a	t
b	c	m	a	r	n	a	s	f	i
u	v	a	n	y	g	x	a	f	d
s	p	e	e	d	l	i	m	i	t
o	p	z	b	p	t	r	u	c	k

On average, up to **EIGHT MOTORBIKES FIT** into the **SAME PARKING SPACE** taken up by **ONE CAR.**

Word Search

```
b  i  c  y  c  l  e  q  g  a
v  x  k  s  x  s  v  m  g  e
a  p  r  p  e  t  r  o  l  w
d  i  n  d  i  c  a  t  o  r
r  o  u  n  d  a  b  o  u  t
i  s  c  o  o  t  e  r  g  x
v  e  h  i  c  l  e  b  p  f
e  r  x  l  e  l  t  i  p  a
r  c  l  a  n  e  s  k  k  w
t  n  s  e  a  t  b  e  l  t
```

MOPEDS get their name because they are **MOTOR-POWERED**, and used to have **PEDALS** like **BICYCLES.**

bicycle
driver
indicator
lanes
motorbike

petrol
roundabout
scooter
seatbelt
vehicle

49

CLOSE UP

Match the mind-boggling magnifications to the named pictures opposite. See if you are right by flicking to page 97.

Bus

1

Taxi

2

Car

3

Van

4

Bike

5

6

Lorry

GUESS WHAT?

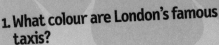

Can you guess the answers to the road transport questions below?
Check your guesses by flicking to page 97.

1. What colour are London's famous taxis?
   a) Yellow
   b) White
   c) Black

2. How does a taxi indicate it is available for hire?
   a) It flashes its headlights
   b) It beeps its horn
   c) It illuminates the light on its roof

3. Approximately how many bus stops are there in London?
   a) 900
   b) 9,000
   c) 19,000

4. Which of these is a bus station in Glasgow?
   a) Barclay Bus Station
   b) Ballantyne Bus Station
   c) Buchanan Bus Station

5. What are two-storey buses called?
   a) Double-deckers
   b) Two-floorers
   c) Double-floorers

6. What type of car has a collapsible roof?
   a) Crumpler
   b) Deflatable
   c) Convertible

7. Approximately how many days of their life are British drivers stuck in traffic?
   a) 9
   b) 49
   c) 99

8. What is cruise control used to maintain?
   a) Speed
   b) Temperature
   c) Pressure

9. Which road has 3 lanes?
   a) A road
   b) B road
   c) Motorway

10. What material is traditionally used to make protective clothing for motorbike users?
    a) Nylon
    b) Cotton
    c) Leather

MAZE

Work your way around the maze until you reach the exit. See if you are right by flicking to page 97.

Word wheels

Can you work out the vehicle words in the two word wheels?
See if you are right by flicking to page 97.

No engine travel

No keys? No problem. Navigate through the next chapter for fun facts and puzzles on engine-less transport.

In the city of **AMSTERDAM,** there are **MORE BICYCLES** than there are **PEOPLE!**

CROSSWORDS

Crack the crosswords to get off to a flying start by solving the cryptic clues below.
Answers have the same amount of letters as the number in brackets.
Can you work out the engine-less transport keyword using the letters in the
shaded squares? See if you are right by flicking to page 98.

Over **1 BILLION**
pairs of **RUNNING**
SHOES are **SOLD**
world-wide **EACH**
YEAR.

Across

1 Very attractive (9)
4 Talk about (7)
6 Join together; link (7)
9 Atmospheric conditions (7)
10 Oblong (9)

Down

1 Do by (anagram) (4)
2 Examine carefully (7)
3 Happening now (of a TV show) (4)
5 Show where a singer performs (7)
7 Polar ___ : large white mammal (4)
8 Opposite of false (4)

SCOOTERS used to be made out of WOOD, but they went out of FASHION!

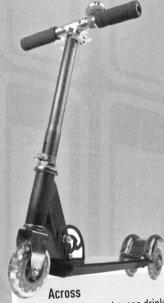

Across

4 Hot ___ : sweet cocoa drink (9)
6 You walk on this (3)
8 In that place (5)
9 E.g. Pacific or Atlantic (5)
10 Nay (anagram) (3)
12 Absolutely necessary (9)

Down

1 Footwear (4)
2 E.g. Asia or Europe (9)
3 Object used to take photographs (6)
5 All (5)
6 The opposite of tight (5)
7 Oily substance (6)
11 Tidy (4)

SUDOKUS

Solve the sudokus to pick up your paddle. Fill in the blank squares so that numbers 1 to 6 appear once in each row, column and 3x2 box. See if you are right by flicking to page 98.

The word **'KAYAK'** means **'HUNTER'S BOAT'** because kayaks were first used to **HUNT FOR FISH AND SEALS.**

1			2		5
		5	6		
4					3
3					
		1	3		
5	3	4		2	6

Puzzle 1:

1	2		3	5	
	5		4		
					1
4					
		5		6	
	3			2	4

Puzzle 2:

		3		5	
	6	3			
6		5	4		
		1	6		
			3	6	
2		6			

Wordsearches

Skate off in search of words. Search left to right, up and down to find the words listed in the boxes below.
See if you are right by flicking to page 98.

bicycle
camel
horse
mule
pony

running
scooter
skateboard
unicycle
walking

BRISK WALKING helps **IMPROVE** your **BLOOD CIRCULATION,** and the **PERFORMANCE** of your **HEART** and **LUNGS.**

q	r	t	z	t	s	j	j	o	l
f	w	w	a	l	k	i	n	g	a
r	u	u	b	h	a	r	m	w	y
u	n	h	i	x	t	a	m	c	x
n	i	o	c	r	e	n	u	r	k
n	c	r	y	u	b	g	l	y	l
i	y	s	c	o	o	t	e	r	p
n	c	e	l	c	a	m	e	l	o
g	l	s	e	c	r	l	c	k	n
g	e	s	t	s	d	l	f	s	y

canoe

dinghy

glider

ice skating

jogging

kayak

pogo stick

rowing

skiing

swimming

g	l	i	d	e	r	r	u	p	s
f	d	c	s	g	x	e	l	r	i
r	i	e	t	i	s	j	o	o	r
e	u	s	c	a	n	o	e	w	m
f	t	k	v	c	y	g	n	i	m
p	k	a	y	a	k	g	i	n	b
j	l	t	s	k	i	i	n	g	t
s	w	i	m	m	i	n	g	p	p
i	t	n	d	i	n	g	h	y	d
p	o	g	o	s	t	i	c	k	e

CLOSE UP

Match the mind-boggling magnifications to the named pictures opposite. See if you are right by flicking to page 99.

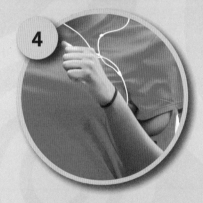

Bicycle

1

Running

2

Scooter

3

Roller skates

4

Canoe

5

Kayak

6

GUESS WHAT?

Can you guess the answers to the engine-less transport questions below? Check your guesses by flicking to page 99.

1. Which of these animals usually pulls a cart?
   a) Sheep
   b) Chicken
   c) Horse

2. How can you travel across deep water without the use of a boat?
   a) Run
   b) Walk
   c) Swim

3. Which of these might you attach to your feet to travel over snow?
   a) Skis
   b) Flip-flops
   c) Flippers

4. Which of these might you use when on ice?
   a) Canoe
   b) Pogo stick
   c) Skates

5. Which of these boats has no engine?
   a) Rowing boat
   b) Speedboat
   c) Cruise ship

6. Which of these modes of transport has three wheels?
   a) Unicycle
   b) Bicycle
   c) Tricycle

7. Which of these is an aircraft designed to fly without using an engine?
   a) Jumbo jet
   b) Glider
   c) Spitfire

8. Which of these is a pace a horse might move at?
   a) Canter
   b) Counter
   c) Chaser

9. What is a benefit of walking rather than driving?
   a) Better for the environment
   b) Takes longer to get to your destination
   c) You might get wet and catch a cold

10. Which of these is an enclosed area for skating?
    a) Rank
    b) Drink
    c) Rink

MAZE

Work your way around the maze until you reach the exit.
See if you are right by flicking to page 99.

Word wheels

Can you work out the engine-free travel words in the two word wheels?
See if you are right by flicking to page 99.

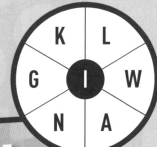

Hitching a ride

Jump on! Trek through this chapter for fun facts and puzzles about our four-legged friends.

In **SOUTH EAST ASIA,** some wealthy people used to travel in expensive 'HOWDAH' carriages on **ELEPHANTS' BACKS.**

CROSSWORDS

Crack the crosswords and gallop off by solving the cryptic clues below.
Answers have the same amount of letters as the number in brackets.
Can you work out the animal transport keyword using the letters in the
shaded squares? See if you are right by flicking to page 100.

Because
HORSES used to
PULL VEHICLES
along, we still use the term
'HORSEPOWER' to
describe an engine's
POWER.

Across
1 Occur (6)
5 Cry noisily (3)
7 How old you are (3)
8 Of great significance (9)
9 We breathe this in (3)
10 Catch sight of (3)
11 A breakfast food usually eaten from a
   bowl with milk (6)

Down
1 Place where ill people are looked after (8)
2 Document you need when going
   abroad (8)
3 Nationality of a person from Tokyo (8)
4 Opposite of horizontal (8)
6 Winged creatures (5)

PONIES are **SMALLER HORSES** that are often used by **CHILDREN** who are **LEARNING TO RIDE.**

Across

1 Speech sound that is not a vowel (9)
5 Sprinted (3)
7 London's location (7)
8 Very big flightless bird (7)
11 Half of two (3)
12 Vanish from sight (9)

Down

1 Thick and strong paper (9)
2 Seven plus two (4)
3 A space or region (4)
4 Cuddly toy (5,4)
6 Once more (5)
9 The end parts of the feet (4)
10 Empty space in an object (4)

SUDOKUS

Help the camel solve the sudokus. Fill in the blank squares so that numbers 1 to 6 appear once in each row, column and 3x2 box. See if you are right by flicking to page 100.

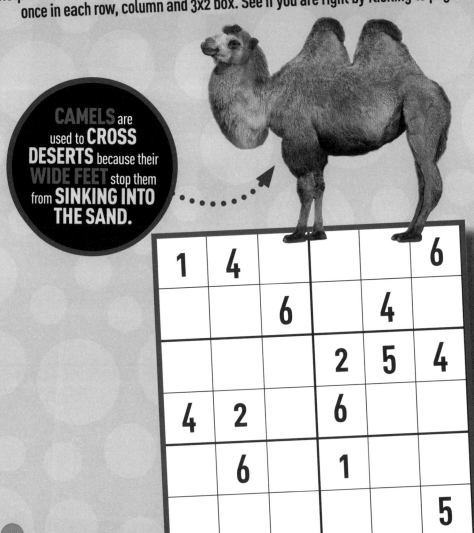

CAMELS are used to **CROSS DESERTS** because their **WIDE FEET** stop them from **SINKING INTO THE SAND.**

1	4				6
		6		4	
			2	5	4
4	2		6		
	6		1		
					5

Puzzle 1

2	6	5			
	1		6		
					3
4	3				
		3	4	6	
			5	3	1

Puzzle 2

4					
3	2	6			5
				6	
	1				
5			3	1	2
				5	6

Wordsearches

Complete the wordsearches with help from the donkey.
Search left to right, up and down to find the words listed in the boxes below.
See if you are right by flicking to page 100.

t	r	n	u	a	n	p	c	g	b
r	s	l	i	f	t	k	a	e	j
a	a	o	s	j	h	o	r	s	e
v	i	r	e	o	w	u	s	v	e
e	b	r	o	u	t	e	h	o	k
l	s	y	r	r	s	a	e	p	
s	l	t	h	n	t	p	r	u	k
p	a	t	i	e	n	c	e	q	p
t	r	e	k	y	u	e	i	t	r
l	e	s	e	r	s	o	a	j	s

The **SEASIDE HOLIDAY** tradition of **DONKEY RIDES** along the beach was started way back in **VICTORIAN TIMES.**

carshare

hike

horse

journey

lift

route

travel

trek

t	a	x	i	l	f	l	i	b	r
g	s	a	a	i	f	r	w	a	a
u	r	w	e	r	d	g	a	c	v
e	o	t	x	k	e	r	n	k	d
b	a	o	p	p	i	a	d	p	o
s	d	u	l	o	s	t	e	a	n
n	s	t	o	u	r	e	r	c	k
s	i	s	r	z	i	f	e	k	e
a	d	v	e	n	t	u	r	e	y
v	e	r	r	a	q	l	f	r	l

adventure
backpacker
donkey
explorer

lost
roadside
tour
wanderer

In some parts of **TIBET, YAKS** are used for more than just **CARRYING GOODS – YAK RACING** is a popular **SPORT!**

Compare the two images of the elephant.
Can you spot the five differences between the images?
See if you are right by flicking to page 101.

Even though they are so **BIG AND STRONG,** it can actually be harmful to elephants to use them for transportation.

GUESS WHAT?

Can you guess the answers to the travel questions below?
Check your guesses by flicking to page 101.

1. Which animal would you traditionally ride at the seaside?
   a) Seal
   b) Donkey
   c) Ape

2. Where would you be most likely to ride a Yak?
   a) Antarctica
   b) Asia
   c) Europe

3. Nomads are likely to travel on which of these animals?
   a) Kangaroo
   b) Camel
   c) Pig

4. What is horsepower used to describe?
   a) Car speed
   b) Engine power
   c) Radio volume

5. What do you sit on when travelling by horse?
   a) A bench
   b) A stool
   c) A saddle

6. What is a male donkey called?
   a) A jack
   b) A peter
   c) A bob

7. Which of these animals transport people across the desert?
   a) Camel
   b) Rhino
   c) Deer

8. Which of these animals can be used to transport goods?
   a) Mule
   b) Chicken
   c) Snake

9. What is a mule?
   a) Offspring of a male donkey and female horse
   b) Offspring of a female donkey and male goat
   c) Offspring of a male zebra and female donkey

10. Where would you be most likely to ride an elephant?
    a) North America
    b) South America
    c) Asia

MAZE

Work your way around the maze until you reach the exit.
See if you are right by flicking to page 101.

Word wheels

Can you work out the animal transport words in the two word wheels?
See if you are right by flicking to page 101.

Wheel 1: O K E N D Y

Wheel 2: H L E P A T E N

In an emergency

Explore this chapter for facts and puzzles on the emergency services.

Before **FIRE ENGINES** had sirens, **DALMATIAN DOGS** and **HORSES** used to run ahead of them to **CLEAR THEIR PATHS.**

CROSSWORDS

Crack the crosswords to start the sirens by solving the cryptic clues below.
Answers have the same amount of letters as the number in brackets.
Can you work out the emergency vehicle keyword using the letters in the
shaded squares? See if you are right by flicking to page 102.

POLICE IN BOLOGNA use **SUPER CARS** for special tasks like transporting **ORGANS.**

Across
1 Very impressive or incredible (9)
5 Animal doctor (3)
7 E.g. is the abbreviation of this word (7)
8 Litter (7)
11 Slippery snake-like fish (3)
12 All people (9)

Down
1 Best-loved (9)
2 Short letter (4)
3 Stumble (4)
4 Cautiously (9)
6 Feeling of alarm (5)
9 The colour of the sky on a clear day (4)
10 Someone you look up to (4)

Sometimes **POLICE OFFICERS** use **MOTORBIKES** instead of **CARS** in order to whizz through traffic more **QUICKLY** and **EASILY.**

Across

4 Large fruit (9)
6 A chicken might lay one (3)
8 Produce a paper copy of a document stored on computer (5)
9 Two times (5)
10 Attempt (3)
12 This follows morning (9)

Down

1 Make musical sounds (4)
2 Small red fruit (9)
3 Run very quickly (6)
5 Way into a place (5)
6 Additional (5)
7 The opposite of innocent (6)
11 The top of a building (4)

SUDOKUS

Solve the sudokus to put out the fire. Fill in the blank squares so that numbers 1 to 6 appear once in each row, column and 3x2 box. See if you are right by flicking to page 102.

See if you are right by flicking to page 102.

The world's first **AMBULANCES** were **SMALL CARTS** pulled along by **HORSES**, or powered by people on **BICYCLES**.

1	5	2			4
	4	6			
	2			1	
	3			2	
			5		
4		5			1

Not all **FIRE ENGINES** are red, in some **COUNTRIES** they might be **GREEN, YELLOW,** or even **WHITE.**

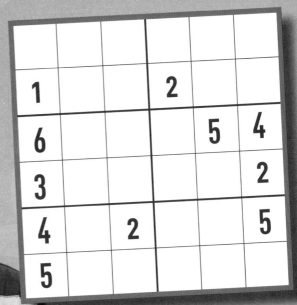

1			2		
6				5	4
3					2
4		2			5
5					

4	5	2			
	1				
			6	2	4
2		6			
			4	5	
			1	6	

Wordsearches

Scramble the search party to complete the wordsearches.
Search left to right, up and down to find the words listed in the boxes below.
See if you are right by flicking to page 102.

air rescue	helicopter
ambulance	lifeboat
coastguard	mine rescue
fire engine	police bike
first aid	speed

In 2017, **ITALIAN FIREFIGHTERS** had to use a **RESCUE HELICOPTER** to airlift a fallen **COW** to **SAFETY.**

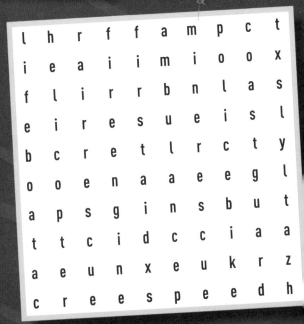

l	h	r	f	f	a	m	p	c	t
i	e	a	i	i	m	i	o	o	x
f	l	i	r	r	b	n	l	a	s
e	i	r	e	s	u	e	i	s	l
b	c	r	e	t	l	r	c	t	y
o	o	e	n	a	a	e	e	g	l
a	p	s	g	i	n	s	b	u	t
t	t	c	i	d	c	c	i	a	a
a	e	u	n	x	e	u	k	r	z
c	r	e	e	s	p	e	e	d	h

alarm
alert
blue light
doctor
lifeguard

police car
rescue team
search team
sirens
stay calm

Since its formation in 1824, the **ROYAL NATIONAL LIFEBOAT INSTITUTION** has **SAVED** more than **140,000 LIVES.**

d	o	c	t	o	r	a	c	l	a
l	i	f	e	g	u	a	r	d	l
e	o	j	a	l	e	r	t	i	a
e	i	o	i	v	w	j	b	r	r
s	e	a	r	c	h	t	e	a	m
r	e	s	c	u	e	t	e	a	m
n	u	s	t	a	y	c	a	l	m
k	i	k	p	s	i	r	e	n	s
p	o	l	i	c	e	c	a	r	o
b	l	u	e	l	i	g	h	t	h

Lifeboats

17-37

SPOT THE DIFFERENCE

Compare the two images of the fire engine.
Can you spot the five differences between the images?
See if you are right by flicking to page 103.

The first organised municipal **FIRE BRIGADE** in the world was the **EDINBURGH** Fire Engine Establishment, formed in **SCOTLAND!**

GUESS WHAT?

Can you guess the answers to the emergency service transport questions below? Check your guesses by flicking to page 103.

1. What is used to alert the public that an emergency vehicle is coming?
   a) An announcement
   b) A siren
   c) A letter

2. Police officers that are undercover use a car that is:
   a) Unmarked
   b) Secret
   c) Disguised

3. What are police cars fitted with so officers can communicate with each other?
   a) Telephones
   b) Radios
   c) Sat navs

4. Where was the first police car used?
   a) Ottawa
   b) Ohio
   c) Oslo

5. What are fire engines fitted with?
   a) Escalators
   b) Elevators
   c) Ladders

6. Which breed of dog is associated with the fire service?
   a) Dalmatian
   b) Spaniel
   c) German Shepherd

7. When was the London Ambulance Service formed?
   a) 1765
   b) 1865
   c) 1965

8. What tanks would you find in an ambulance?
   a) Hydrogen
   b) Nitrogen
   c) Oxygen

9. What lifeboat charity was founded in 1824?
   a) Royal National Lifeboat Institution
   b) Her Majesty's National Lifeboat Institution
   c) His Majesty's National Lifeboat Institution

10. Which emergency vehicle would rescue people on mountains?
    a) Lifeboat
    b) Helicopter
    c) Fire engine

MAZE

Work your way around the maze until you reach the exit. See if you are right by flicking to page 103.

Word wheels

Can you work out the emergency vehicles in the two word wheels?
See if you are right by flicking to page 103.

Solutions

Crosswords

```
S O M E T I M E S
U   I         I   E
B I N   B   S   V
S   T H E A T R E
T   L         N   N
A I R P O R T   T
N   O W   U S E
C   O         N   E
E N T E R T A I N
```

Keyword: AEROPLANE

```
A C C E N T
L   O       C   I
P   M A N   O W N
H   P   I   N   C
A L L I G A T O R
B   E   H   I   E
E A T   T I N   A
T   E       U   S
      B R E E Z E
```

Keyword: CABLE CAR

Sudokus

5	4	1	6	2	3
6	3	2	5	4	1
2	1	4	3	6	5
3	5	6	2	1	4
4	6	3	1	5	2
1	2	5	4	3	6

3	6	2	4	1	5
4	1	5	2	6	3
5	3	4	6	2	1
1	2	6	3	5	4
2	4	1	5	3	6
6	5	3	1	4	2

2	6	3	5	4	1
4	5	1	3	2	6
1	2	6	4	3	5
5	3	4	6	1	2
6	4	2	1	5	3
3	1	5	2	6	4

Wordsearches

```
s s o g c l t d s o
a e g l i d e r b u
e a b l l a l o u s
r p p x d i r n t k
o l q p i r a e t i
p a j u m b o j e t
l n o a o u w p r e
a e m g t s l r f j
n e b u h r r q l e
e s s a a l e t y j
```

```
r b a l l o o n f e
r s p a c e s h i p
y o r s r t v d g b
e p b l i m p a h j
y p a r a c h u t e
h e l i c o p t e r
e a g l e g t r r d
g b h t i w t c j c
h a n g g l i d e r
i t x r o c k e t d
```

Page 14–15

Spot the difference

Page 16–17

Guess what?

1) a – Helipad 2) b – Aeroplane 3) a – Spaceship

4) a – Cockpit 5) b – Drone 6) c – Chopper

7) b – Red, white and blue 8) c – Engines

9) a – Hovering 10) b – Wright brothers

Maze

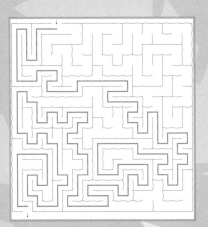

Word wheels

Glider, Helicopter

Solutions

Crosswords

Crossword 1:

F	R	A	N	C	E		
R		T		A	C	S	
I	N	T	E	R	R	U	P	T
G		E			R		R
H	A	N	D		U	R	G	E
T		D			E		S
E	L	E	P	H	A	N	T	S
N		D		A		C		E
			S	T	A	Y	E	D

Keyword: FERRY

Crossword 2:

A	F	R	I	C	A		
S		E		O		M		S
T	E	M	P	O	R	A	R	Y
O		E				T		M
N	A	M	E		S	T	O	P
I		B				R		A
S	P	E	E	D	I	E	S	T
H		R		Y		S		H
			J	E	R	S	E	Y

Keyword: YACHT

Sudokus

Sudoku 1:

1	5	3	6	4	2
6	2	4	3	1	5
2	4	1	5	3	6
3	6	5	1	2	4
4	3	6	2	5	1
5	1	2	4	6	3

Sudoku 2:

5	2	6	3	4	1
1	3	4	6	2	5
4	1	2	5	3	6
6	5	3	4	1	2
3	6	1	2	5	4
2	4	5	1	6	3

Sudoku 3:

4	5	3	6	2	1
1	6	2	5	4	3
3	2	1	4	5	6
5	4	6	3	1	2
6	1	5	2	3	4
2	3	4	1	6	5

Wordsearches

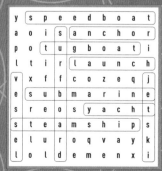

Close Up

Page 26-27

1 – 3 Junk ship   2 – 1 Hovercraft   3 – 5 Cruise ship

4 – 2 Yacht   5 – 6 Fishing boat   6 – 4 Jet ski

Guess what?

Page 28-29

1) a – Periscope   2) c – Hull

3) c – Dock   4) a – Kayak

5) c – Mast   6) b – Stern

7) c – Cargo ship   8) b – RMS Titanic

9) c – Submarine   10) a – Dinghy

Maze

Word wheels

Hovercraft, Yacht

Solutions

Page 32–33

Crosswords

C	R	O	C	O	D	I	L	E	
R		W			R			X	
O	I	L		E		O		C	
S		S	T	R	A	N	G	E	
S				R				L	
W	E	L	C	O	M	E		L	
O			O		R	L	I	E	
R		A			S			N	
D	I	F	F	E	R	E	N	T	

Keyword: STEAM

		C		C				V	
S	H	O	R	T	S			O	
		E		E		T	E	L	L
		M		A		R		U	
H	I	N	T		A	U	N	T	
		S		U		N		E	
S	T	A	R		N		E		
		R	E	L	E	V	E	N	
		Y			R			R	

Keyword: TRAIN

Page 34–35

Sudokus

6	4	2	3	1	5
1	5	3	6	2	4
5	1	4	2	6	3
2	3	6	4	5	1
3	2	1	5	4	6
4	6	5	1	3	2

6	1	5	3	4	2
4	3	2	6	5	1
5	2	1	4	3	6
3	4	6	1	2	5
1	5	3	2	6	4
2	6	4	5	1	3

1	2	4	5	3	6
6	5	3	4	1	2
3	6	2	1	4	5
4	1	5	2	6	3
2	3	1	6	5	4
5	4	6	3	2	1

Page 36–37

Wordsearches

s	t	p	r	e	p	b	b	p	d
s	r	c	a	b	l	e	c	a	r
t	a	a	i	m	a	i	u	s	i
a	m	r	l	o	n	t	s	s	v
t	l	r	w	n	f	u	b	e	e
i	e	i	a	o	o	w	b	n	r
o	t	a	y	r	r	o	w	g	r
n	l	g	a	a	m	k	a	e	i
t	b	e	a	i	b	r	y	r	a
y	e	s		s	l	e	y	t	s

r	k	t	p	u	r	u	s	a	s
a	s	z	s	r	l	c	t	s	o
q	c	w	e	c	v	o	e	p	y
i	w	q	s	i	g	n	a	l	f
t	u	n	n	e	l	d	m	t	q
r	j	d	w	n	g	u	a	r	d
a	b	s	q	g	d	c	o	a	l
c	m	r	n	i	i	t	y	v	t
k	p	a	t	n	m	o	t	o	r
s	m	o	k	e	p	r	h	o	n

94

Spot the difference

Guess what?

1) a – Take payment, check tickets and help passengers

2) c – Carriages   3) c – Electricity   4) a – Mart (tram)

5) b – 'All aboard!'   6) c – Tunnel   7) a – Tracks

8) a – Station   9) c – Signals

10) a – Stephenson's Rocket

Maze

Word wheels
Monorail, Train

Solutions

Crosswords

```
O N W A R D S   N
V   E     E   E
E   T   H A V O C
R   H   E   E   E
T H E S A U R U S
U   P   R   A   S
R O O M S   L   A
N   O       A   R
S   H O L I D A Y
```

Keyword: CARS

```
G L O S S A R Y
E   P     E   P
N E E D S   L   R
E   R   H O U S E
R   A   I   C   D
O F T E N   T   A
U   I   E X A C T
S   S O     N   O
  A N T E A T E R
```

Keyword: TAXI

Sudokus

2	1	5	3	6	4
3	6	4	1	2	5
6	4	3	5	1	2
1	5	2	6	4	3
4	3	1	2	5	6
5	2	6	4	3	1

4	5	3	2	6	1
2	1	6	5	4	3
3	2	4	6	1	5
1	6	5	4	3	2
6	3	2	1	5	4
5	4	1	3	2	6

5	6	2	3	1	4
4	3	1	6	5	2
2	4	6	1	3	5
3	1	5	2	4	6
1	2	4	5	6	3
6	5	3	4	2	1

Wordsearches

```
a a t c i c o a c h
t i s y a r i b r u
n o p c e o a x m e
p t o l l s r s t b
e i i e m s a k r j
r y e l o i t t a t
b c m a r n a s f i
u v a n y g x a f d
s p e e d l i m i t
o p z b p t r u c k
```

```
b i c y c l e q g a
v x k s x s v m g e
a p r p e t r o l w
d i n d i c a t o r
r o u n d a b o u t
i s c o o t e r g x
v e h i c l e b p f
e r x l e l t i p a
r c l a n e s k k w
t n s e a t b e l t
```

Close Up

1 – 3 Car	2 – 4 Van
3 – 1 Bus	4 – 2 Taxi
5 – 6 Lorry	6 – 5 Bike

Guess what?

1) c – Black
2) c – It illuminates the light on its roof
3) c – 19,000
4) c – Buchanan Bus Station
5) a – Double-deckers
6) c – Convertible
7) c – 99
8) a – Speed
9) c – Motorway
10) c – Leather

Maze

Word wheels

Lorry, Motorbike

Solutions

Page 56–57

Crosswords

Grid 1:

```
B E A U T I F U L
O         N     I V
D I S C U S S     I
Y     O   P       V
  C O N N E C T   E
B     C   C       T
E   W E A T H E R
A     R           U
R E C T A N G L E
```

Keyword: RUNNING

Grid 2:

```
  S     C     C
C H O C O L A T E
  O     N   M   V
L E G     T H E R E
O   R     I   R   R
O C E A N   A N Y
S   A     E   E
E S S E N T I A L
    E T           T
```

Keyword: SCOOTER

Page 58–59

Sudokus

1	6	3	2	4	5
2	4	5	6	3	1
4	1	2	5	6	3
3	5	6	4	1	2
6	2	1	3	5	4
5	3	4	1	2	6

1	2	4	3	5	6
3	5	6	4	1	2
5	6	3	2	4	1
4	1	2	6	3	5
2	4	5	1	6	3
6	3	1	5	2	4

4	1	2	3	6	5
5	6	3	1	2	4
6	2	5	4	1	3
3	4	1	6	5	2
1	5	4	2	3	6
2	3	6	5	4	1

Page 60–61

Wordsearches

Grid 1:

```
q r t z t s j j o l
f w w a l k i n g a
r u u b h a r m w y
u n h i x t a m c x
n i o c r e n u r k
n c r y u b g l u l
i y s c o o t e r p
n c e l c a m e l o
g l s e c r l c k n
g e s t s d l f s y
```

Grid 2:

```
g l i d e r r u p s
f d c s g x e l r i
r i e t i s j o o r
e u s c a n o e w m
f t k v c y g n i m
p k a y a k g i n b
j l t s k i i n g l
s w i m m i n g p p
i t n d i n g h y d
p o g o s t i c k e
```

98

Page 62-63

Close Up

1 – 3 Scooter   2 – 1 Bicycle   3 – 5 Canoe

4 – 2 Running   5 – 6 Kayak   6 – 4 Roller skates

 Page 64-65

Guess what?

1) c – Horse   2) c – Swim   3) a – Skis

4) c – Skates   5) a – Rowing boat 6) c – Tricycle

7) b – Glider   8) a – Canter

9) a – Better for the environment   10) c – Rink

Maze

Word wheels

Running, Walking

Solutions

Crosswords

Crossword 1

```
H A P P E N
O   A     J V
S   S O B   A G E
P   S   I   P   R
I M P O R T A N T
T   O   D   N   I
A I R   S E E   C
L   T     S     A
    C E R E A L
```

Keyword: HORSE

Crossword 2

```
C O N S O N A N T
A   I       R   E
R A N   A   E   D
D   E N G L A N D
B       A       Y
O S T R I C H   B
A   O   N   O N E
R   E       L   A
D I S A P P E A R
```

Keyword: PONY

Sudokus

1	4	3	5	2	6
2	5	6	3	4	1
6	3	1	2	5	4
4	2	5	6	1	3
5	6	4	1	3	2
3	1	2	4	6	5

2	6	5	3	1	4
3	1	4	6	2	5
5	2	6	1	4	3
4	3	1	2	5	6
1	5	3	4	6	2
6	4	2	5	3	1

4	5	1	6	2	3
3	2	6	1	4	5
2	4	3	5	6	1
6	1	5	2	3	4
5	6	4	3	1	2
1	3	2	4	5	6

Wordsearches

Wordsearch 1

```
t r n u a n p c g b
r s l i f t k a e j
a a o s j h o r s e
v i r e o w u s v e
e b r o u t e h o k
l s y r r r s a e p
s l t h n t p r u k
p a t i e n c e q p
t r e k y u e i t r
l e s e r s o a j s
```

Wordsearch 2

```
t a x i l f l i b r
g s a a i f r w a a
u r w e r d g a c v
e o t x k e r n k d
b a o p p i a d p o
s d u l o s t e a n
n s t o u r e r c k
s i s r z i f e k e
a d v e n t u r e y
v e r r a q l f r l
```

100

Spot the difference

Guess what?

1) b – Donkey   2) b – Asia   3) b – Camel

4) b – Engine power   5) c – A saddle   6) a – A jack

7) a – A camel   8) a – Mule

9) a – Offspring of a male donkey and female horse

10) c – Asia

Maze

Word wheels

Donkey, Elephant

Solutions

Crosswords

Crossword 1:

F	A	N	T	A	S	T	I	C
A		O		R			A	
V	E	T		P	I		R	
O		E	X	A	M	P	L	E
U				N			F	
R	U	B	B	I	S	H		U
I		L		C		E	E	L
T		U			R			L
E	V	E	R	Y	B	O	D	Y

Keyword: AMBULANCE

Crossword 2:

		S		R		S		
P	I	N	E	A	P	P	L	E
		N		S		R		N
E	G	G		P	R	I	N	T
X		U		B		N		R
T	W	I	C	E		T	R	Y
R		L		R		O		
A	F	T	E	R	N	O	O	N
		Y		Y		F		

Keyword: POLICE

Sudokus

Sudoku 1:

1	5	2	3	6	4
3	4	6	1	5	2
5	2	4	6	1	3
6	3	1	4	2	5
2	1	3	5	4	6
4	6	5	2	3	1

Sudoku 2:

2	6	4	5	1	3
1	5	3	2	4	6
6	2	1	3	5	4
3	4	5	1	6	2
4	1	2	6	3	5
5	3	6	4	2	1

Sudoku 3:

4	5	2	3	1	6
6	1	3	2	4	5
1	3	5	6	2	4
2	4	6	5	3	1
3	6	1	4	5	2
5	2	4	1	6	3

Wordsearches

Wordsearch 1:

l	h	r	f	f	a	m	p	c	t
i	e	a	i	i	m	i	o	o	x
f	l	i	r	r	b	n	l	a	s
e	i	r	e	s	u	e	i	s	l
b	c	r	e	t	l	r	c	t	y
o	o	e	n	a	a	e	e	g	l
a	p	s	g	i	n	s	b	u	t
t	t	c	i	d	c	c	i	a	a
	a	e	u	n	x	e	u	k	r	z
c	r	e	e	s	p	e	e	d	h

Wordsearch 2:

d	o	c	t	o	r	a	c	l	a
l	i	f	e	g	u	a	r	d	l
e	o	j	a	l	e	r	t	i	a
e	i	o	i	v	w	j	b	r	r
s	e	a	r	c	h	t	e	a	m
r	e	s	c	u	e	t	e	a	m
n	u	s	t	a	y	c	a	l	m
k	i	k	p	s	i	r	e	n	s
p	o	l	i	c	e	c	a	r	o
b	l	u	e	l	i	g	h	t	h

Spot the difference

Guess what?

1) b – A siren
2) a – Unmarked
3) b – Radios
4) b – Ohio
5) c – Ladders
6) a – Dalmatian
7) c – 1965
8) c – Oxygen
9) a – Royal National Lifeboat Institution
10) b – Helicopter

Maze

Word wheels

Ambulance, Lifeboat

Look for more puzzle books in this series!

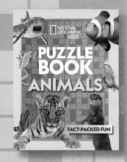